# Aguas Frescas & PALETAS

Refreshing Mexican Beverages and Frozen Treats,
Traditional and Reimagined

Published by Familius LLC, www.familius.com
PO Box 1249 Reedley, Ca 93654.

Familius books are available at special discounts for bulk purchases,
whether for sales promotions or for family or corporate use.
For more information, contact Familius Sales at orders@familius.com.

Library of Congress Control Number: 2020950046

Print ISBN  9781641704595
Ebook ISBN 9781641705073
KF 9781641705271
FE 9781641705479

Printed in China

Edited by Ashlin Awerkamp and Peg Sandkam
Cover and book design by Mara Harris

10 9 8 7 6 5 4 3 2

First Edition

*To my son, Joaquin, and my nieces, Sophia and Frida,
for bringing so much sweetness into my life.*

# CONTENTS

## PALETAS

# INTRODUCTION

**M**y love of aguas frescas and paletas began at my grandmother Amelia's house in Torreón, Coahuila, Mexico. My summer ritual was to spend my elementary school vacation at her bodega-like family-owned specialty convenience store, *Miscelánea Dulce*. We sold everything, from small bags of laundry detergent to *pan dulce* to sugar and rice by the kilo.

We spent the early hours of the day in the rear of the store, which was also her house, concocting different fruit mixtures to sell as either a beverage or a frozen treat. Instead of using molds to freeze the sweetened fruit mixtures, we poured them in small plastic bags and tied each in a knot. We called them *gallinitas*, or "little hens," because their shape resembled the body of a small, plump hen. Our best customers were children walking home from school. A thin paper napkin protected their small hands from the cold burn of the frozen bag of flavored ice. They bit off the plastic bag tip and gradually chewed out bits of the cold, sweet treat until it was all gone, making the walk home under the hot Coahuila sun a refreshing one.

These fruit-flavored treats have always been part of my life, since the time I lived in Mexico to growing up in Texas to now living in California. In my kitchen, *flor de jamaica* (dried hibiscus flowers), tamarind pods, rice, and frozen fruit pulp are staples, always there to refresh our day either in beverage or frozen form.

Now I get to share with you a variety of my favorite traditional aguas frescas and paletas flavors. Some I learned years ago at my grandmother's store. Others are new and inspired by my Mexican travels and California's abundance of easily accessible produce.

# DEFINITIONS

*Aguas frescas* are mixtures of water, sweetener (mainly sugar), and seasonal fruit pulp. The fruit might be blended, crushed, chopped, or strained. The recipes in this book are nonalcoholic with the exception of the fermentation in *tepache* and the sherry cooking wine in *paletas de nogada*. Aguas frescas are usually served cold, with minimal ice—only a few degrees cooler than room temperature. They are inexpensive and an excellent method of avoiding food waste. Many Mexican households and restaurants choose to enjoy aguas frescas with afternoon or evening meals. Stands throughout Mexico vividly display a rainbow of fruit-flavored drinks in large transparent glass *vitroleros,* or jugs. Some are ladled into disposable plastic or Styrofoam cups, others in plastic bags fastened by a knot or a tightly wound rubber band accompanied by a large straw. Different areas in Mexico have their own regional favorites. Some of the most popular flavors in Mexico and the United States include horchata, tamarind, hibiscus, and lemon chia.

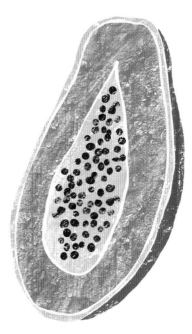

If you have aguas frescas, you also have paletas. *Paletas,* or ice pops, are frozen versions of aguas frescas. Some have a water, juice, or milk base, and they are generally frozen with a plastic or wooden stick to serve as a handle. Paletas are sold throughout Mexico at *paleterias,* ice pop shops, ice cream parlors, and mobile ice cream carts equipped with loud steel bells jingled by vendors called *paleteros.* Now paletas can be found everywhere in the frozen foods section of favorite grocery stores, though most of those are artificially colored and flavored.

## SWEETENERS
///////////////////

In the majority of the recipes in this book, I use pure cane sugar. If pure cane sugar is not available, granulated sugar (beet sugar) will work just as well. Both pure cane and granulated sugar are the sweeteners of choice in aguas frescas stands and ice pop shops in Mexico. In a few other recipes, I use dark brown sugar, honey, piloncillo, raw agave syrup, cream of coconut, sweetened condensed milk, dulce de leche, or *cajeta* (sweetened caramelized goat's milk). Of course, you can always use your preferred sweetener and adjust the amount to your liking. When making paletas, taste the mixture before pouring it into the mold and make any necessary changes. Keep in mind that the sugar needs to dissolve completely before adding the mixture to the mold.

## EQUIPMENT
///////////////////

Equipment is minimal in making homemade aguas frescas and paletas. A high-powered blender is essential to puree fruit. A metal strainer also helps keep purees smooth by eliminating seeds and pulp fibers. A large pitcher (one that holds at least twelve cups, or three liters), a large spoon with a long handle for stirring, and a citrus squeezer will certainly make preparation easy.

To make most of these paleta recipes, I use one to two standard ten-slot reusable pop makers. Each slot measures approximately 3.5" x 2" x 1" and makes a three-ounce pop. The mold comes with a lid equipped with grommets to hold standard wooden sticks upright. If you are not able to get your hands on a frozen pop mold, use three-ounce disposable paper cups. Some fun molds of different shapes and sizes can be found online and in stores that sell kitchenware. Most molds come with a set of sticks, or you can find them at craft stores or online. I went through hundreds of wooden sticks when developing and testing these paleta recipes, so don't hesitate to buy plenty.

To fill your molds, use a pitcher with a spout. Please keep in mind that liquid expands when frozen; leave at least a one-third-inch space on top of each mold or disposable cup.

To unmold your paletas, follow the mold's manufacturer's instructions. You can also run the molds under warm water for 20 seconds, continuously pulling on the sticks until the paletas are released. You can also dip the bottom of the mold in a large bowl filled with warm water. For paletas frozen in disposable cups, simply tear off the cup and enjoy.

To store your paletas after removing them from the mold, stack them two or three deep, using parchment paper to keep them from sticking to each other. Carefully place them in a large freezer bag and chill. Paletas keep well for two or three weeks.

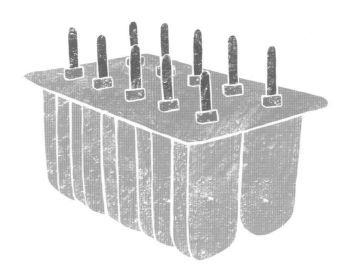

# AGUAS FRESCAS

# HORCHATA

## [Agua de Horchata]

*Serves 6*

### INGREDIENTS:
////////////////////////

1 cup uncooked white rice
1 (4-inch) cinnamon stick
4 cups water
1½ teaspoons vanilla extract
½ cup milk
⅓ cup + 2 tablespoons
   granulated sugar
¼ tablet (11.25 grams)
   Mexican chocolate

### DIRECTIONS:
////////////////////////

Soak rice and cinnamon stick in water overnight.

Transfer the soaked rice, cinnamon stick, and water to a blender. Blend until smooth.

Add vanilla, milk, sugar and Mexican chocolate. Blend again. Serve over ice.

At any taqueria or aguas frescas stand, you are sure to find a giant jug of *agua de horchata*. Made with rice, cinnamon, water, and vanilla, this ice-cold beverage is the best accompaniment to the spiciest salsa-drenched tacos. Everyone has their own favorite version of this drink, and this is mine. I add a bit of milk and Mexican chocolate to give it a richer flavor, and that makes all the difference.

# CANTALOUPE COOLER
## [Agua de Melón]

One of my most vivid memories from my summer vacations is strolling down the Alameda, a plaza in downtown Torreón filled with street vendors, shoe shiners, and kiddie carnival rides. The agua de melón at the plaza's agua fresca stand was the sweetest and most refreshing drink. I still remember the sound of the ice pick breaking down the ice of the colorful fruit-infused glass barrels. The few pesos I earned at my grandmother's convenience store would never cover my purchase, but my *tío* Roman happily helped me out.

I haven't visited la Alameda in over twenty years, but I re-create my own version of that agua de melón as soon as cantaloupe hits its peak season. You will find the sweetest, freshest cantaloupes between June and August.

*Serves 8*

### INGREDIENTS:
////////////////////////

1 ripe cantaloupe
8 cups water, divided
½ cup pure cane sugar

### DIRECTIONS:
////////////////////////

Slice cantaloupe in half and scoop out seeds. (You can reserve them for Cantaloupe Seed Horchata; see page 28.)

Slice pulp into large pieces and place in blender. Add 2 cups water and blend until smooth.

Transfer blended cantaloupe to a pitcher. Add remaining 6 cups water and sugar. Stir until the sugar dissolves. Serve over ice.

# ALFALFA LIME COOLER

## [Agua de Alfalfa y Lima]

*Serves 8*

### INGREDIENTS:
//////////////////////

2 cups (packed) rinsed alfalfa
¾ cup lime juice
¾ cup pure cane sugar
8 cups water, divided

### DIRECTIONS:
//////////////////////

Combine alfalfa, lime juice, sugar, and 4 cups water in blender. Blend until smooth.

Transfer to a pitcher and add remaining 4 cups water. Stir. Serve chilled or over ice.

I was five years old the first time I ever tried alfalfa lime agua fresca. It was during a family trip to visit la Torre Latinoamericana in the historic center of Mexico City. We stopped at an aguas frescas stand, and I chose the deep green drink thinking it was limeade. It looked so vibrant and refreshing, and it was love at first sip. Now, every time I see alfalfa on my grocery trips, I have to snatch up a couple of bunches and create my own version of this thirst-quenching drink I so vividly remember.

# HIBISCUS & SPICED ORANGE COOLER

## [Agua de Jamaica y Naranja con Especias]

*Serves 8*

**M**y friend Nicole gave me the great idea of adding orange slices with whole cloves to my hibiscus and orange agua fresca. The infusion of clove spice and orange peel elevated it to a completely different type of drink. It reminds me of autumn, something an agua fresca has never reminded me of. With that in mind, I served this drink at our Thanksgiving feast, and everyone loved it. Needless to say, this will be the drink of choice every Thanksgiving from now on.

### INGREDIENTS:

7 cups water, divided
1½ cups dried hibiscus flowers
20 whole cloves

3 oranges, sliced
¾ cup pure cane sugar
2 cups freshly squeezed orange juice

### DIRECTIONS:

Combine 3 cups water and hibiscus flowers in a medium saucepan. Bring to a boil over medium heat for 2 minutes. Remove from heat and set aside to steep and cool for 15 minutes.

While tea cools, insert 3 or 4 cloves in each orange slice. Set aside.

Combine sugar and remaining 4 cups water in a serving pitcher. Stir to dissolve sugar.

Once tea has cooled, strain mixture into a large bowl. Save some hibiscus for garnish. (Reserve the rest to cook for another time; store in a tightly sealed container in the refrigerator.)

Add cooled hibiscus tea, orange juice, and orange slices with cloves to the pitcher of sugar water. Chill in refrigerator or serve immediately over ice. Garnish with hibiscus flowers.

# JAMAICA (HIBISCUS)

*Jamaica*, or hibiscus, is sour and a dark red color when dry. It is used dehydrated to prepare an infusion to make *agua de jamaica*, one of the most consumed aguas frescas in Mexico. It's usually sold in bulk in markets and packaged in grocery stores.

# FERMENTED PINEAPPLE PEEL COOLER

## [Tepache]

**INGREDIENTS:**

8 cups water
1 large ripe organic pineapple

1 (8-ounce) piloncillo cone
2 whole cloves
2 (4-inch) cinnamon sticks

**DIRECTIONS:**

Heat water in a large 5-quart pot over medium heat for 5 to 7 minutes. Do not boil. Remove from heat.

While water heats, wash pineapple thoroughly. Using a brush, remove any dirt or debris on the peel. Cut off and discard crown. Slice off peel lengthwise in large strips and set them aside. (Store pineapple flesh for use elsewhere.)

Add piloncillo, cloves, and cinnamon sticks to hot water. Stir until piloncillo dissolves.

Transfer mixture to a large glass jar. Add pineapple peel. Cover with a cheese cloth secured with a rubber band.

Keep in a dry area at room temperature for 2 to 5 days or until desired taste. (Taste and stir daily, making sure pineapple peel is completely submerged in water.)

Discard solids. Serve over ice and enjoy. Keep refrigerated.

*Serves 6-8*

**S**old in small clay *jarritos* (little jars) on the streets of Mexico and at taco stands, tepache is a tart and sweet fermented drink with only trace amounts of alcohol. The main ingredient is pineapple peel. The fermentation takes a few days, and the process is simple, calling for few ingredients. The result is a kombucha-like pineapple and cinnamon flavor.

# PAPAYA & MANGO COOLER

## [Agua de Papaya y Mango]

One of the greatest things about living in Los Angeles is that most people are lucky enough to have a fruit tree nearby. When my husband and I purchased our first home, we had three beautiful papaya trees in our backyard. They were tall and abundant with fruit. The problem was once the papayas were ripe, they fell and splattered all over our back patio. After the first couple of years, we had to pay more attention and pick them ahead of time. The fruit would then finish ripening on our kitchen counter. Once we figured out how to identify the best time to bring down those coveted papayas, we made papaya and mango agua fresca for the entire season. Keep a pitcher full of this tropical cooler—you'll want plenty.

*Serves 10*

### INGREDIENTS:
////////////////////////////

2 cups chopped papaya

1 cup frozen mango pulp, thawed

⅔ cup raw honey

6 cups water, divided

3 tablespoons lime juice

### DIRECTIONS:
////////////////////////////

Combine papaya, mango pulp, honey, and 2 cups water in a blender. Blend until smooth.

Transfer to a pitcher. Stir in remaining 4 cups water and lime juice. Serve over ice.

# CHAYOTE COOLER
## [Agua de Chayote]

*Serves 8*

### INGREDIENTS:

6 cups water, divided
¼ cup + 2 tablespoons raw honey
3 chayote squash (about 6 cups)
2 tablespoons lime juice
⅛ teaspoon (pinch) salt

### DIRECTIONS:

Place 5 cups water in a large pitcher. Add honey and stir to dissolve. Set aside.

Deseed and chop chayote squash. Place squash and remaining 1 cup water in a blender. Blend until smooth.

Run mixture through a strainer into sweetened water pitcher, scraping and pressing juice with a spoon.

Stir in lime juice and salt. Serve over ice.

Chayote (pronounced *chai-yo-te*) is a warm climate fruit that resembles a pear but is cooked like a squash. It can be baked, stuffed, added to salads, turned into a soup, and, yes, made into an invigorating agua fresca. The flavor, like a cucumber, is mild and fresh.

# STRAWBERRY ALMOND HORCHATA

## [Horchata de Almendra y Fresa]

*Serves 12*

Once I discovered the simple process of making my very own almond milk, I was excited to make homemade strawberry almond horchata. My secret time-saving tip is using slivered raw almonds instead of whole. No more peeling almonds! Once soaked and blended, their consistency is creamy and lightly starchy— perfect for a strawberry almond horchata.

### INGREDIENTS:
///////////////////////

1 pound slivered almonds, raw and peeled
8 cups water, divided
1 teaspoon ground cinnamon

8 cups (2½ pounds) whole strawberries, divided
1 cup pure cane sugar

### DIRECTIONS:
///////////////////////

Soak almonds in 4 cups water overnight.

Add soaked almonds, almond water, and cinnamon to a blender. Blend on high for 1 minute.

Run mixture through a fine strainer into a large pitcher, pressing mixture against the strainer with a large spoon.

Hull and roughly chop strawberries. Reserve 2 cups. Add the rest of the strawberries and 1 cup water to blender. Blend on high until smooth. Add mixture to pitcher.

Stir in sugar. Add remaining 3 cups water and the reserved chopped strawberries. Stir. Serve over ice.

# PLUM COOLER
## [Agua de Ciruela]

*Serves 4*

INGREDIENTS:
///////////////////////

6 plums, pits removed
6 cups water
⅓ cup raw agave syrup

DIRECTIONS:
///////////////////////

Chop the plums. Place all ingredients in a blender. Blend until smooth. Strain into a pitcher. Serve over ice.

When making plum agua fresca, make sure those plums are at the peak of their season, usually around midsummer. The flesh is sweeter and juicier, and removing the pit is ten times easier. All you have to do is slice the fruit down the middle and twist each side in opposite directions. With the help of a small paring knife, carefully carve around the pit and scoop it out.

# CANTALOUPE SEED HORCHATA

## [Horchata de Pepita de Melón]

**D**on't discard those cantaloupe seeds after making cantaloupe agua fresca. You can make an entirely new horchata beverage by using the seeds as the main ingredient. Their grit gives this agua fresca the starchy consistency we love in an horchata drink.

*Serves 4-6*

### INGREDIENTS:

seeds from a large cantaloupe (about ¾ cup)
4 cups water
1 teaspoon vanilla extract
¼ cup raw agave syrup

### DIRECTIONS:

Blend all ingredients until smooth. Run mixture through a strainer into a pitcher. Place mixture back in the blender and blend again for 10 seconds. Strain into pitcher. Serve over ice.

# CUCUMBER CHIA LIMEADE

## [Agua de Pepino, Lima, y Chia]

*Serves 6-8*

### INGREDIENTS:
////////////////////////

2 cucumbers, divided
6 cups water, divided
1 cup pure cane sugar

½ cup lime juice
2 tablespoons chia seeds
lime slices for garnish

### DIRECTIONS:
////////////////////////

Chop 1½ cucumbers into large pieces. Reserve the rest for garnish.

Place cucumber pieces, 1 cup water, and sugar in blender. Blend until smooth. Transfer mixture to serving pitcher.

Stir in remaining 5 cups water, lime juice, and chia seeds.

Using a peeler, make thin cucumber strips out of the remaining cucumber half. Divide between serving glasses. Add ice, then add drink. Garnish with lime slices and serve.

This limeade with hints of cucumber will keep you hydrated during the hottest days. Not only is it citrusy and thirst-quenching, but it also includes a superfood: chia! Use your favorite type of cucumber and make plenty. You'll love how invigorating it is.

# CHIA

Chia is a seed native to Mexico. It's mainly
added to cold drinks such as lemonade and,
more recently, yogurt bowls and breakfast
smoothies. When hydrated, the seeds have
a gelatinous consistency. It is considered an
antioxidant and is rich in fiber.

# MINT BLACKBERRY LEMONADE

## [Limonada de Mora y Menta]

*Serves 8*

### INGREDIENTS:
////////////////////

½ cup pure cane sugar
5 cups water, divided
1½ cups lemon juice
3 cups blackberries

2 tablespoons (packed) fresh mint, plus a few sprigs for garnish

### DIRECTIONS:
////////////////////

Place sugar and 1 cup water in a small saucepan over medium heat. Stir until sugar has dissolved. Set aside to cool.

Combine lemon juice, blackberries, and mint in a blender. Blend until smooth.

Place sugar water mixture and remaining 4 cups water in a large pitcher. Stir in blackberry mixture, with or without running it through a strainer.

Serve cold or over ice and garnish with mint sprigs.

**B**lackberries are a delicious way to give traditional lemonade an antioxidant berry twist. This lemonade is the ideal drink to serve at spring celebrations, picnics, and family get-togethers. Want to give it a little fizz? Add a splash of club soda.

# GUAVA & CINNAMON COOLER

## [Agua de Guayaba y Canela]

*Serves 6*

### INGREDIENTS:
//////////////////////

8 Mexican cream guavas, divided
6 cups water, divided
1½ teaspoons ground cinnamon
6 tablespoons raw honey

### DIRECTIONS:
//////////////////////

Slice ends off 6 guavas, then cut each in half. Scoop out seeds with a small spoon. Place guavas in blender with 3 cups water, cinnamon, and honey. Blend until smooth.

Run mixture through a strainer into a pitcher. Stir in remaining 3 cups water.

Slice remaining 2 guavas into wedges. Add wedges to pitcher. Serve over ice.

Mexican cream guavas are very fragrant and sweet. I get so excited when they are in season because I know the holidays are right around the corner. Customarily, I enjoy guavas in my Christmas punch or as a dessert cooked in piloncillo and cinnamon syrup, also known as *guayabas en almibar*. This agua fresca is a fresher take on the creamy tropical fruit. It's cool and comforting and perfect to enjoy with spicy enchiladas or a smoky black Christmas mole.

# MANDARIN WITH GINGER & CHIA COOLER

## [Agua de Mandarina con Jengibre y Chia]

*Serves 6*

**M**andarins abound in our home. We buy them in large quantities because they make great snacks and fit perfectly in a lunch box. Combined with fresh ginger and chia seeds, they make a delightful beverage you can enjoy at any time of the day. We like our agua de mandarina slightly sweetened with agave syrup, but you can use your favorite sweetener or omit it completely.

### INGREDIENTS:

2 cups water, divided
1 tablespoon chia seeds
2 tablespoons raw agave syrup (optional)
3½ cups freshly squeezed mandarin juice (about 25 small mandarins)

1½ tablespoons roughly chopped fresh ginger
mandarin slices for garnish

### DIRECTIONS:

Combine ¼ cup water and chia seeds in a small bowl. Set aside to hydrate.

Place remaining 1¾ cups water and agave syrup in a large pitcher. Stir to mix well.

Place mandarin juice and ginger in a blender. Blend until smooth.

Add juice mixture and hydrated chia seeds to pitcher and stir. Serve cold or over ice and garnish with mandarin slices.

# WATERCRESS PINEAPPLE COOLER

## [Agua de Berros y Piña]

*Serves 4*

### INGREDIENTS:

2 cups (packed) rinsed watercress
2 cups roughly chopped pineapple
¾ cup pure cane sugar
6 cups water, divided

### DIRECTIONS:

Combine watercress, pineapple, sugar, and 3 cups water in blender. Blend until smooth.

Transfer to a pitcher and add remaining 3 cups water. Stir. Serve cold or over ice.

Next time you visit the farmers' market, pick up a watercress bunch and blend it with sweet pineapple. The acid in the pineapple and the spice of the watercress create the most invigorating combination of flavors.

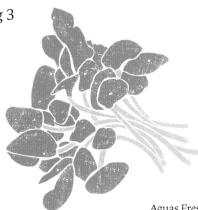

# MINTY RED PRICKLY PEAR & RASPBERRY COOLER

## [Agua de Tuna Roja con Menta y Frambuesa]

*Serves 6-8*

Around the time I was ten years old, Sundays always meant a family day trip to Ciudad Juárez, Chihuahua. It was only a fifteen-minute car ride from our home in El Paso, Texas. We spent the day going to mass, having breakfast, getting haircuts, and going to the *mercado* (market).

The car ride back over the border wasn't as quick. We patiently inched our way to the front of the crossing line, sometimes waiting two to three hours. To keep the kids happy, my parents would buy us a bag filled with peeled and chilled *tunas*, or prickly pears. These juicy gems kept us cool and content during the long car ride home and were a treat we always looked forward to.

My mom would also buy extra bags to make agua fresca with at home. Not having to peel the prickly pears herself was a time-saver for my mother; the tiny spines were almost impossible to remove from fingers when one got pricked.

Now I make my own prickly pear agua fresca with the addition of raspberries and a few mint leaves. It's an amazing flavor combination your family is going to love.

### INGREDIENTS:

6 red prickly pears, peeled
1 cup raspberries
2 tablespoons fresh mint, some leaves reserved for garnish

2 teaspoons lime juice
4 cups water
½ cup pure cane sugar
lime slices for garnish

### DIRECTIONS:

Place prickly pears and raspberries in a blender. Blend until smooth.

Run mixture through strainer, pressing the juice out with a spoon. Discard seeds.

Return juice to the blender. Add mint and lime juice. Blend again for 10 seconds.

Combine water and sugar in a pitcher. Stir until sugar dissolves.

Run juice through strainer into the pitcher. Mix well by stirring with a large spoon. Garnish with mint leaves and lime slices, and serve over ice.

# OATCHATA
## [Horchata de Avena]

*Serves 6-8*

## INGREDIENTS:

7 cups water, divided
1 cup rolled oats
1 (4-inch) cinnamon stick

1½ cups evaporated milk
1 cup pure cane sugar
1 teaspoon vanilla extract

## DIRECTIONS:

Heat 3 cups water in a large saucepan over medium heat for about 5 minutes. Do not boil. Remove from heat. Add oats and cinnamon stick. Set aside for 30 minutes.

Place 1 cup water in blender. Add softened cinnamon stick from saucepan and blend on high until smooth. Run cinnamon water through a strainer into a pitcher. Set aside.

Place soaked oats with their water in blender. Blend on high until smooth. Add blended oats to pitcher with cinnamon water.

Add remaining 3 cups water, evaporated milk, sugar, and vanilla to pitcher. Stir until sugar dissolves. Serve over ice.

I consider my son, Joaquin, horchata's number one fan. He requests it every week with his meals. But when I am short on time, he asks for the "quick horchata": oatchata, made with rolled oats. The rolled oats give it that iconic starchy, creamy, horchata flavor we all love. No rice and no overnight soaking is needed because it can be prepared while cooking your meal.

# GRAPEFRUIT & ALOE COOLER

## [Agua de Toronja y Sábila]

My house is surrounded by aloe vera plants, and every time grapefruits are in season, we make this grapefruit aloe agua fresca. All we do is take a paring knife, head to the backyard, and slice off a piece of the aloe plant. The combination of the sweet-acidic taste of the grapefruit, the bitterness of the aloe juice, and the sweetness of honey makes this tasty drink perfect any time of the day.

*Serves 6*

### INGREDIENTS:

½ cup aloe vera pulp
2 cups fresh grapefruit juice (about 2 grapefruits)
⅓ cup raw honey
3 cups water

### DIRECTIONS:

Combine all ingredients in a blender. Blend until smooth. Serve over ice.

# GREEN PRICKLY PEAR & SPINACH COOLER

## [Agua de Tuna Verde y Espinacas]

*Serves 8*

### INGREDIENTS:
///////////////////////

10 green prickly pears, peeled and roughly chopped
1 cup baby spinach
6 cups water, divided
¾ cup pure cane sugar
¼ cup lime juice
*arils* (seeds) from 1 pomegranate

### DIRECTIONS:
///////////////////////

Combine prickly pears, baby spinach, and 2 cups water in blender. Blend until smooth.

Place remaining 4 cups water and sugar in pitcher. Stir until sugar has dissolved.

Run prickly pear mixture through a strainer into the pitcher. Stir in lime juice.

Serve over ice. Decorate with pomegranate *arils*.

*Agua de tuna*, or prickly pear agua fresca, is a drink served at restaurants and in homes in Mexico. Because prickly pears flourish in Mexico and South America, it's very common and very popular. Whether red or green, this sweet and juicy fruit is included in salads, desserts, and syrups. It's delicious right off the cactus too, but one must be careful when peeling and removing the spines.

For this green prickly pear agua fresca, I added spinach to intensify the beautiful green color and the health benefits.

# *TUNA* (PRICKLY PEAR)

Green or red, *tuna* (prickly pear) is an oval-shaped fruit with thick skin and small spines. Its interior is filled with a fleshy, soft, and sweet pulp and lots of edible seeds. It is consumed fresh, mashed, added to salsas, or cooked into a thick syrup.

# STRAWBERRY ORANGE BEET COOLER

## [Agua de Fresa, Naranja, y Betabel]

*Serves 12*

**B**eets didn't enter my life until I was in my midtwenties. I never paid attention to them until the time my mom made beet agua fresca. Its vibrance and magenta hue caught my eye immediately. My mom wouldn't tell me what it was until I tried it. I was pleasantly surprised when she told me what it was. It was so sweet and delicious, and I was mad at myself for not trying it before. Now I am making up for lost time and preparing beets any way I can.

If you are introducing beets to your family, this agua fresca is the perfect way to do it. The beet taste is not overpowering, and the strawberries and orange juice add a familiar flavor everyone will love.

### INGREDIENTS:

1 medium red beet
2 cups strawberries, hulled
6 cups water, divided
⅔ cup pure cane sugar
1¼ cups freshly squeezed orange juice

### DIRECTIONS:

Place beet in a medium saucepan with enough water to cover the beet. Boil over medium heat for 1 hour.

Remove from heat, drain hot water, and set beet aside to cool. Once cool, peel with a paring knife and cut into large pieces.

Combine beet pieces, strawberries, and 1 cup water in a blender. Blend until smooth. Strain mixture into a large pitcher.

Stir in sugar, orange juice, and remaining 5 cups water. Serve cold or over ice.

# PINEAPPLE CUCUMBER BASIL COOLER

## [Agua de Piña, Pepino, y Albahaca]

*Serves 16*

### INGREDIENTS:

1 medium pineapple
1 cucumber (about 1¾ cups)
⅓ cup (packed) fresh basil leaves
¼ cup + 2 tablespoons pure cane sugar
7 cups water

### DIRECTIONS:

Peel and chop pineapple and cucumber. Place chunks in a blender. Blend until smooth.

Add basil and sugar. Blend for 10 more seconds.

Transfer mixture to a large pitcher and stir in water. Serve over ice.

The combination of pineapple and basil might sound a bit strange, but once you try it, the flavor will knock your socks off. I went a step further and added cucumber to the mix, and the drink just keeps getting better. Serve it as a brunch beverage or at an outdoor spring gathering.

# PALETAS

# RICE PUDDING POPS
## [Paletas de Arroz con Leche]

*Makes 10*

### INGREDIENTS:
//////////////////////

2½ cups water, divided
⅓ cup short grain rice, rinsed
1 (12 ounces) can evaporated milk
⅔ cup pure cane sugar
½ teaspoon ground cinnamon

### DIRECTIONS:
//////////////////////

Boil 1½ cups water in a medium saucepan over medium heat. Add rice. Cover and cook on low for 20 minutes or until rice is tender and most of the water has been absorbed. Remove from heat.

Add remaining 1 cup water, evaporated milk, sugar, and cinnamon to cooked rice. Stir to combine ingredients.

Spoon mixture into popsicle molds. Cover and insert popsicle sticks. Freeze at least 4 hours or until firm.

These paletas take me back to those summery Sunday strolls at La Plaza Las Margaritas in Torreón, Coahuila. The weather was too warm for a comforting bowl of *arroz con leche*, so this frozen version of the classic Mexican dessert was just as enjoyable. They are creamy, cinnamony, and bursting with plump, tender rice.

# CLASSIC LIME POPS
## [Paletas de Lima]

*Makes 10*

The classic lime paletas are the paletas of my childhood. Now my son loves them too. They are the perfect balance of sweet and tart in every bite—the perfect cooling treat for kids. Making them is just as easy as making lemonade. Don't pass these up in the hot summer!

### INGREDIENTS:
///////////////////////

½ cup pure cane sugar
3 cups water
¾ cup lime juice

### DIRECTIONS:
///////////////////////

Combine sugar and water in large pitcher. Stir until sugar dissolves completely. Stir in lime juice.

Pour mixture into popsicle molds. Cover and insert popsicle sticks. Freeze at least 4 hours or until firm.

# HIBISCUS WATERMELON POPS
## [Paletas de Jamaica y Sandia]

*Makes 16*

### INGREDIENTS:
//////////////////////////

1 cup dried hibiscus flowers
1½ cups water
5 cups roughly chopped watermelon
½ cup pure cane sugar

### DIRECTIONS:
//////////////////////////

Combine hibiscus flowers and water in medium bowl. Soak for 1 hour. Strain into blender and discard used hibiscus flowers.

Add watermelon and sugar to blender. Blend until smooth.

Add mixture to popsicle molds. Cover and insert popsicle sticks. Chill overnight.

*F*lor de jamaica, or dried hibiscus flowers, can be found at any Latin market. When steeped and sweetened, it's a tart, punchy drink that's aromatic and invigorating. With the addition of fresh watermelon, these paletas are the epitome of summer on a stick.

# MEXICAN CHOCOLATE POPS

## [Paletas de Chocolate Mexicano]

*Makes 10*

When the temperature rises and it's too hot for a frothy cup of Mexican chocolate, freeze it! For all the chocoholics out there, this is the paleta for you. It's luscious, fudgy, creamy, and rich in authentic Mexican chocolate flavor.

### INGREDIENTS:

3 cups milk
3 tablespoons cornstarch
¼ cup cocoa powder

1 tablet (90 grams) Mexican chocolate
⅛ teaspoon salt
½ cup sweetened condensed milk

### DIRECTIONS:

Combine milk and cornstarch in large saucepan over medium heat. Whisk continuously until mixture comes to a boil and cornstarch dissolves. Remove from heat.

Whisk in cocoa, Mexican chocolate, and salt. Stir in sweetened condensed milk. Mixture should be thick.

Spoon mixture into popsicle molds. Cover and insert popsicle sticks. Freeze at least 4 hours or until firm.

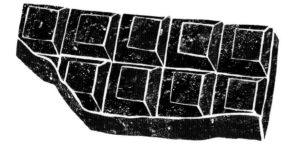

# MEXICAN CHOCOLATE

Mexican chocolate, or Mexican drinking chocolate, can be found in tablet or ground form in major supermarkets, usually in the Latin section. The most common variety is the coarse combination of cacao, sugar, and cinnamon. Some varieties include ground almonds and vanilla. Mexican chocolate's rich, smoky flavor enhances mole sauces and other traditional drinks such as *atole* and *champurrado*. It is most commonly dissolved in hot water or milk and enjoyed frothy.

# AVOCADO COCONUT POPS

## [Paletas de Coco y Aguacate]

*Makes 8*

### INGREDIENTS:
////////////////////////

1 large avocado, roughly chopped
½ cup canned coconut milk
1 cup oat milk
½ cup pure cane sugar
3 tablespoons sweetened coconut flakes

### DIRECTIONS:
////////////////////////

Combine avocado, milks, and sugar in a blender. Blend until smooth.

Pour mixture in popsicle molds, filling three-fourths of the way up. Divide coconut flakes between cups. Cover and insert popsicle sticks. Freeze at least 4 hours or until firm.

In Mexico, avocado isn't just for guacamole. The avocado pulp can also be made into a rich and delicious dessert. Because of its creamy consistency, avocado has the perfect texture to be made into a frozen treat. The addition of other ingredients—such as cocoa, pistachio, or coffee—makes it one of the most versatile ingredients for paletas. To create this decadent tropical treat, I added coconut.

# MANGO & CHAMOY POPS
## [Paletas de Mango y Chamoy]

*Makes 10*

Go to any *frutero*, or street fruit vendor, and you will surely find *mangonadas*. Also known as *chamangos*, this summer favorite is made with fresh mangoes, mango puree, or mango sorbet and enhanced with chamoy. The combination of flavors is heavenly. Chamangos are traditionally served as a drink, but we are transforming them into a frozen treat.

### INGREDIENTS:
//////////////////////

3 cups Ataulfo mango (about 5 mangoes), divided
2 tablespoons freshly squeezed lime juice

½ cup pure cane sugar
¼ cup water
2 tablespoons chamoy sauce
1 teaspoon chili lime salt

### DIRECTIONS:
//////////////////////

Add 2½ cups mango, lime juice, sugar, and water to blender. Blend until smooth. Set aside ⅔ cup of mango mixture.

Place the rest of the mango mixture in a small bowl. Stir in chamoy sauce and chili lime salt.

Chop remaining ½ cup mango into half-inch cubes.

Divide mango cubes into popsicle molds. Layer plain mango mixture and chamoy mango mixture in each mold, alternating between mixtures. Push mixtures in the mold with a spoon to make swirls. Cover and insert popsicle sticks. Chill overnight.

# CHAMOY

Chamoy is a chili sauce made with salt, sugar, and pickled fruit such as apricots and tamarind. It's eaten with fruits, such as mangoes and oranges, and potato chips. Chamoy is sold in Latin markets and packaged in large plastic bottles.

# CORN POPS
## [Paletas de Elote]

*Makes 10*

### INGREDIENTS:

2 cups milk
1 (4-inch) cinnamon stick
3 cups yellow corn kernels
⅓ cup cream cheese

¾ cup sweetened
    condensed milk
1 teaspoon vanilla extract

### DIRECTIONS:

Heat milk and cinnamon stick in a medium saucepan over medium-low heat for 8 minutes. Do not boil.

Stir in corn and cream cheese. Continue stirring until cream cheese has mostly melted.

Add sweetened condensed milk. Bring to a boil. Remove from heat.

Stir in vanilla. Let cool. Discard cinnamon stick.

Place mixture in blender. Pulse 5 or 6 times or blend until smooth.

Pour into popsicle molds. Cover and insert popsicle sticks. Freeze at least 4 hours or until firm.

The use of corn in Mexican cuisine is endless. Not only is it used in traditional savory foods, such as corn tortillas or the beloved street corn on the cob, but it is also one of the most popular flavors in Mexican paleterias. The sweetness of fresh corn and the creaminess of sweetened condensed milk create the perfect indulgence for those with a sweet tooth.

# TRICOLOR POPS: KIWIFRUIT, COCONUT, & WATERMELON

## [Paletas Tricolor: Kiwi, Coco, y Sandia]

**T**hese tricolor paletas, also called *bandera* paletas (flag pops), are modeled after the Mexican flag. These colorful paletas are popular during *fiestas patrias*—Mexican Independence Day on September 16 and the weeks in September leading up to the big festivities. The layers of kiwifruit, coconut, and watermelon are very distinct. This paleta is three desserts rolled into one.

*Makes 12*

## INGREDIENTS:
//////////////////////

**Green layer**
4 kiwifruit, peeled
   and halved
2 tablespoons pure
   cane sugar
2 tablespoons water

**White layer**
¼ cup cream of coconut
1 cup milk
¼ teaspoon vanilla extract

**Red layer**
2 cups roughly
   chopped watermelon
2 tablespoons pure
   cane sugar

## DIRECTIONS:
//////////////////////

**Green layer.** Combine kiwifruit, sugar, and water in blender. Blend until smooth. Divide mixture between popsicle molds. Cover, insert popsicle sticks, and chill in freezer for at least 4 hours.

**White layer.** Combine cream of coconut, milk, and vanilla extract in blender. Blend for 10 seconds. Divide mixture between molds over frozen green layer. Cover and chill in freezer for at least 4 hours.

**Red layer.** Combine watermelon and sugar in blender. Blend until smooth. Divide mixture between molds over frozen white layer. Cover and chill in freezer for at least 4 hours.

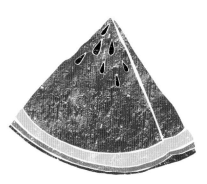

# ORANGE & YOGURT POPS

## [Paletas Ensueño de Naranja]

**F**rozen pops for breakfast? Why not! These orange and cream paletas are made with a Greek yogurt base and fresh orange juice. Add some plump pieces of orange wedge and it's a frozen smoothie on a stick.

*Makes 12*

### INGREDIENTS:

1 cup freshly squeezed orange juice
1 cup vanilla Greek yogurt
½ teaspoon vanilla extract
½ cup pure cane sugar
1 orange, peeled and chopped in quarter-inch pieces

### DIRECTIONS:

Whisk together all ingredients until creamy. Pour into popsicle molds. Cover and insert popsicle sticks. Freeze at least 4 hours or until firm.

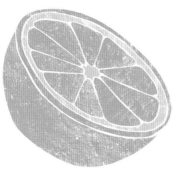

# TAMARIND POPS
## [Paletas de Tamarindo]

*Makes 16*

### INGREDIENTS:
///////////////////////

15 tamarind pods
8 cups water, divided

1¼ cups pure cane sugar

### DIRECTIONS:
///////////////////////

Remove tamarind shells and fibers by hand.

Heat peeled tamarind pods and 4 cups water in a medium saucepan over medium heat. Bring to a boil. Reduce heat to medium-low and simmer for 15 minutes. Remove from heat.

Mash tamarinds to a lumpy paste with potato masher. Stir in 2 cups water. Run through a strainer into blender.

While straining, press mixture with a spoon to extract as much pulp and juice as possible. Discard any fibers, membranes, and seeds.

Add remaining 2 cups water and sugar to blender. Blend until smooth.

Pour mixture into popsicle molds. Cover and insert popsicle sticks. Freeze at least 4 hours or until firm.

Tamarind is a podlike fruit with a tart brown pulp. In Mexico, chili powder and sugar are added to the pulp to make a popular candy with a flavor unlike any other. The pulp is so versatile that it is used to make sauces and marinades as well. My favorite way to enjoy tamarindo is in refreshing drinks and frozen treats. These pops are a staple at every paleteria and aguas frescas stand and are the best treat to enjoy any day.

# TAMARIND

Tamarind belongs to the legume family. It has rough brown bark, a somewhat fibrous brown pulp, and large seeds. Its flavor is sweet and sour. Tamarind is very common throughout Mexico, especially in the warm regions where it is grown. The fruit is bought fresh to be eaten as a candy. It also serves to prepare *agua de tamarindo*, one of the most common flavors of agua fresca in Mexico. Tamarind is usually sold at Latin and Asian markets.

# COCONUT LIME POPS
## [Paletas de Coco y Lima]

I best describe these coconut lime paletas as a frozen coconut cream pie with a citrus twist. They are creamy, rich, and the best way to refresh and satisfy your sweet tooth.

*Makes 10*

### INGREDIENTS:

2 cups milk
1 teaspoon vanilla extract
½ cup cream of coconut
¼ cup sweetened coconut flakes
¼ cup lime juice
zest of 1 lime

### DIRECTIONS:

Place all ingredients in a blender. Blend until smooth.

Pour mixture into popsicle molds. Cover and insert popsicle sticks. Freeze at least 4 hours or until firm.

# STRAWBERRY TRES LECHES POPS

## [Paletas de Tres Leches y Fresa]

*Makes 6-8*

### INGREDIENTS:
//////////////////////

2 cups chopped
    strawberries
½ cup granulated sugar
1 tablespoon lemon juice

1 cup milk
1 cup evaporated milk
¾ cup sweetened
    condensed milk

### DIRECTIONS:
//////////////////////

Combine strawberries, sugar, and lemon juice in a medium saucepan over medium heat. Cook for 12 minutes, stirring every 2 minutes, until strawberries are soft and mixture resembles jam. Remove from heat and set aside to cool.

Combine milks in a blender. Blend for 10 seconds.

Divide strawberry mixture between popsicle molds. Add tres leches mixture. Cover and insert popsicle sticks. Freeze at least 4 hours or until firm.

Every time I make a homemade tres leches cake, my son asks me to decorate it with fresh strawberries. I decided to do the same when I came up with these creamy tres leches paletas. Topped with a layer of sweet, fresh strawberry marmalade, these creamy treats are pleasing not only to the eye but to the palate too.

# BANANA CAJETA POPS
## [Paletas de Plátano y Cajeta]

*Makes 20*

These pops are a great way to use up leftover ripe bananas. The addition of cajeta swirls gives it a special deep, rich flavor that's one of the most popular flavors in my family.

### INGREDIENTS:

1 cup evaporated milk
1 cup sweetened condensed milk
1 cup table cream

1 teaspoon vanilla extract
6 ripe bananas, divided
⅓ cup cajeta, divided

### DIRECTIONS:

Combine milks, table cream, vanilla, and 4 bananas in blender. Blend until smooth.

Slice remaining bananas. Place 3 or 4 slices in each popsicle mold. Add approximately 1 teaspoon cajeta to each mold.

Add milk mixture to molds, shaking gently and filling in any air pockets. Cover and insert sticks. Freeze overnight.

# CAJETA

Cajeta is goat's milk candy. It's a very thick liquid prepared with sugar, baking soda, and cornstarch. The ingredients are boiled with milk for several hours in a copper saucepan until the mixture thickens and takes on a light brown color. If cajeta is not available, dulce de leche is an excellent replacement.

# CANTALOUPE CUCUMBER POPS

## [Paletas de Melón y Pepino]

*Makes 12*

### INGREDIENTS:

5 cups chopped cantaloupe
¼ cup raw honey

½ cup finely chopped cucumber, divided
chili lime salt (optional)

### DIRECTIONS:

Combine cantaloupe and honey in a blender. Blend until smooth.

Place 1 teaspoon cucumber pieces in each popsicle mold. Pour in cantaloupe and honey mixture, filling three-fourths of the way up.

Divide the rest of the cucumber pieces into each mold. Cover and insert popsicle sticks. Freeze at least 4 hours or until firm.

Remove from freezer. Take pops out of mold, sprinkle with chili lime salt (optional), and enjoy.

There is something about shopping at the vendor carts around town that makes their fruit taste so good to me. Maybe it's the entire process of witnessing the *frutero* quickly peel, chop, and slice cantaloupe and cucumber into perfect long slivers and tightly fit them in a plastic cup. Maybe it's the way they season the fruit with an abundance of hot sauce, chili salt, and lime juice. Whatever it may be, I enjoy the fruit every time I purchase a cup.

Now I get to create that joy at home in frozen form when I prepare these cantaloupe cucumber paletas. The bits of cucumber frozen in sweet cantaloupe juice is a fresh treat all street fruit lovers will thoroughly appreciate.

# CHILI LIME SALT

Chili lime salt is a powdered seasoning made with seven types of chili, lime, and salt. It's served as a fruit and vegetable topping to enhance flavor.

# BURNT MILK POPS WITH PECANS

## [Paletas de Leche Quemada con Nuez]

*Makes 12*

The first time I had a *leche quemada* treat was at an ice cream stand inside Oaxaca's Mercado 20 de Noviembre (a well-known Oaxacan market). *Leche quemada* literally means "burnt milk." Whole milk is boiled until it reaches a rich nut taste. Adding sugar transforms its essence into that of dulce de leche. I wanted to capture this flavor in a paleta. It's heavenly. For texture and extra nuttiness, I added pecans to the mix.

### INGREDIENTS:

6 cups whole milk, divided
½ cup dark brown sugar
½ cup pure cane sugar
½ teaspoon ground cinnamon
2 whole cloves
⅓ cup finely chopped pecans

### DIRECTIONS:

Place 1 cup milk in a small saucepan over medium heat. Bring to a boil. Reduce heat to low and simmer for 15 to 20 minutes or until milk curdles and begins to change to a yellowish color, stirring frequently.

Place remaining 5 cups milk in a large saucepan. Bring to a boil. Reduce heat to low.

Add curdled milk, sugars, cinnamon, and cloves to boiled milk. Simmer on low for 15 minutes, stirring frequently. Remove from heat and let cool completely.

Run mixture through a strainer into large pitcher with spout. Stir in pecans.

Divide mixture into popsicle molds. Cover and insert sticks. Chill overnight.

# CAFÉ DE OLLA POPS
## [Paletas de Café de Olla]

*Makes 8*

### INGREDIENTS:
//////////////////////

2 cups water
2 tablespoons chopped piloncillo
1 (4-inch) cinnamon stick

4 tablespoons instant coffee granules
7 tablespoons table cream
24 coffee beans (optional)

### DIRECTIONS:
//////////////////////

Combine water, piloncillo, and cinnamon stick in a medium saucepan. Bring to a boil. Stir until piloncillo dissolves. Remove from heat. Discard cinnamon stick.

Stir in coffee granules. Let cool to room temperature. Once cool, whisk in table cream one tablespoon at a time.

Divide coffee beans between popsicle molds. Pour in mixture, filling three-fourths of the way up. Cover and insert popsicle sticks. Freeze at least 4 hours or until firm.

**C**afé de olla (coffee from the pot) is a cinnamon-spiced coffee drink sweetened with piloncillo. It's sweet but strong and is traditionally prepared in a clay pot. It's perfect in the winter accompanied by pan dulce and great conversation.

Now we can enjoy café de olla during the hot summer months. If you are a fan of coffee drinks or desserts, this is the paleta for you. Just like the hot drink, these can pack a caffeine punch.

# PILONCILLO

Piloncillo, also known as panela or panocha, is a traditional Mexican sweetener in the form of a cone. Dark brown with a similar taste as molasses, piloncillo is made from unrefined sugar. If piloncillo is not available, you can use dark brown sugar.

# GUAVA & COCONUT POPS

## [Paletas de Guayaba y Coco]

When we bought our first house in Los Angeles, the selling point for me was the guava tree that grew right under the balcony that overlooked the city. The guavas' discernible fragrance became stronger as they reached the peak of their season. We had an abundance of guavas to enjoy. Some we ate right off the tree, others I preserved, and most I used to prepare these paletas. A coconut water base makes these tasty paletas a crowd favorite.

*Makes 20*

### INGREDIENTS:

14 guavas, divided
3 cups coconut water
4 large strawberries

⅔ cup pure cane sugar
1 cup sweetened
 coconut shreds

### DIRECTIONS:

Chop 10 guavas (about 3½ cups) into large pieces.

Combine chopped guava, coconut water, and strawberries in a blender. Blend until smooth. Add sugar and blend again until sugar has dissolved.

Place 1 teaspoon coconut shreds in each popsicle mold.

Slice remaining 4 guavas into thin rounds. Place 1 or 2 slices in each popsicle mold.

Fill molds with guava mixture. Divide the remaining coconut shreds between molds. Cover and insert popsicle sticks. Freeze at least 4 hours or until firm.

# NOGADA POPS
## [Paletas de Nogada]

*Makes 12*

### INGREDIENTS:
//////////////////////

2 cups whole milk, divided
1 tablespoon cornstarch
1½ cups heavy whipping
  cream
1 cup sugar
⅛ teaspoon sea salt
2 ounces (about ¼ cup)
  cream cheese
3.9 ounces (about ½ cup)
  soft goat cheese

½ teaspoon ground
  cinnamon
½ cup walnuts or pecans,
  finely chopped
1 teaspoon pecan or
  hazelnut extract
2 teaspoons sherry
  cooking wine or
  1 teaspoon sherry extract
*arils* from 1 large
  pomegranate

### DIRECTIONS:
//////////////////////

Combine ⅓ cup milk and cornstarch; stir until cornstarch dissolves. Set aside.

Combine remaining 1⅔ cups milk, cream, sugar, and salt in a large saucepan over medium heat. Bring to a simmer, stirring frequently. Add cornstarch mixture and bring to a full boil. Continue stirring until mixture thickens, about 5 minutes. Remove from heat.

Mix in cheeses with a handheld mixer for 3 minutes until cheeses dissolve completely and mixture becomes thick and creamy. Set aside and let cool for 15 minutes.

Once cool, stir in cinnamon, nuts, nut extract, sherry, and pomegranate arils.

Pour mixture into popsicle molds. Cover and insert popsicle sticks. Freeze at least 4 hours or until firm.

During *fiestas patrias* season in Mexico (between late summer and early fall), chiles en nogada is a popular traditional food. This labor-intensive dish originated in the state of Puebla by nuns wanting to honor and impress the Mexican Army general Agustín de Iturbide after he signed the Treaty of Córdoba.

To make chiles en nogada, an egg-battered poblano pepper is stuffed with a mixture of ground meat, fruit, and spices. The pepper is topped with a creamy white nogada sauce made with milk, cream, cheese, sherry, and walnuts. The sauce gets its name from *nogal*, Spanish for "walnut tree." The whole thing is then accented with bright red pomegranate arils. The colors of this dish reflect the colors of the Mexican flag.

Although the dish is very traditional, making a dessert out of nogada sauce is not. In recent years, *paletas de nogada* and *helado de nogada* have begun to pop up in *neverias* across Mexico. Now you can make your own at home.

# PERSIMMON AMARANTH POPS

## [Paletas de Caqui y Amaranto]

*Makes 8*

When I see persimmons in the produce section, I get excited because that means autumn, my favorite season, is here. Persimmons are silky and sweet. You can add them to salads, make them into jams, or bake them into loaves and cookies. I decided to make a frozen dessert out of these autumn beauties. Made with coconut milk, sweetened with maple syrup, and accented with bits of puffed amaranth, these sweet vegan treats scream autumn.

### INGREDIENTS:

3 ripe persimmons, peeled and roughly chopped
⅔ cup canned coconut milk
⅔ cup oat milk (or any plant-based milk)
2 tablespoons maple syrup
⅛ teaspoon ground nutmeg
½ cup puffed amaranth, divided

### DIRECTIONS:

Combine persimmon, milks, maple syrup, and nutmeg in a blender. Blend until smooth.

Set aside 1 tablespoon amaranth and divide the rest between popsicle molds.

Pour persimmon mixture into molds, filling three-fourths of the way up. Stir persimmon mixture and amaranth in each mold with a popsicle stick.

Divide the remaining tablespoon of amaranth on top of the filled molds. Cover and insert popsicle sticks. Freeze at least 4 hours or until firm.

# AMARANTH

Amaranth is considered an ancient grain and a superfood. It is gluten-free and high in protein. Cultivated by the Aztecs thousands of years ago, amaranth was added to ritual drinks and foods for energy. Now we toast and pop it like popcorn and add it to our smoothies, salads, and yogurt. Puffed amaranth can be found in specialty stores or online.

# ACKNOWLEDGMENTS

This book would not have come to life without the support of my family. Thank you, Efrain, for all your encouragement and help with this project. You are a wonderful husband, father, and friend. You have given me the space to work and grow, and here we are! You made another one of my many dreams come true. I am the luckiest woman to have you as my partner. Thank you, also, to my number one taste-tester, kitchen helper, and thoughtful son, Joaquin. I love your enthusiasm in the kitchen and excitement for tasting something new. I love you both more than anything in this world.

*Gracias, Mamá,* for all your *consejos,* for always cheering me on, for igniting those *ganas* that keep me going, and for never letting me give up on my dreams. Thank you for all your help in the kitchen and all that dishwashing! Thank you for answering those late-night calls filled with questions and replying to those random odd-hour texts about ingredients and recipes. *Te amo.*

Telma, Aaron, Sophie, and Frida, thank you for the countless support you've provided throughout the years.

Nicole, thank you for keeping me sane with your friendship, enthusiasm, vital feedback on this project, and all the props you've gifted me. You truly are a wonderful friend. We will continue to do great things together.

Celeste, thank you for your friendship, thoughtfulness, help with Joaquin, and your mint bouquet deliveries from your garden.

To the Nibbles and Feasts audience, thank you for your messages of support and encouragement these past ten years. I would've never imagined that my passion for sharing my family's recipes on a website would lead to something extraordinary. *¡Mil gracias!*

Thank you to the entire Familius team, especially Brooke Jorden, managing editor, and Ashlin Awerkamp, my editor, for your guidance with helping me share my vision; Ashley Mireles, sales manager, for believing in me and finding me; and Christopher Robbins, founder and president, for the opportunity to make my dream come true.

# ABOUT THE AUTHOR

Ericka Sanchez is a recipe developer, food stylist, and the creator of the award-winning culinary website nibblesandfeasts. com. Ericka's cooking style is inspired by her life as a bicultural Latina living in California and her cherished memories in the kitchen with her grandmother and mother in Mexico. Ericka was born in Torreón Coahuila, Mexico, and immigrated with her family to El Paso, Texas, at eight years old.

# ABOUT FAMILIUS

**Visit Our Website: www.familius.com**

Familius is a global trade publishing company that publishes books and other content to help families be happy. We believe that the family is the fundamental unit of society and that happy families are the foundation of a happy life. We recognize that every family looks different, and we passionately believe in helping all families find greater joy. To that end, we publish books for children and adults that invite families to live the Familius Nine Habits of Happy Family Life: *love together, play together, learn together, work together, talk together, heal together, read together, eat together,* and *laugh together.* Founded in 2012, Familius is located in Sanger, California.

**Connect**

Facebook: www.facebook.com/paterfamilius
Twitter: @familiustalk, @paterfamilius1
Pinterest: www.pinterest.com/familius
Instagram: @familiustalk

FAMILIUS

*The most important work you ever do will be within the walls of your own home.*